THE BUSINESS SUCCESS GUIDE TO CRICKET FARMING

Sustainable Insect Protein Production, Nutrient-Rich Livestock Feed, Techniques, Nutrition, For Beginners And Experts

RICHMOND HAMILL

© 2024 [RICHMOND HAMILL]. All rights reserved.

Except for brief quotations included in critical reviews and certain other noncommercial uses allowed by copyright law, no part of this book may be reproduced, distributed, or transmitted in any form or by any means, including photocopying, recording, or other electronic or mechanical methods, without the publisher's prior written permission.

Disclaimer

The information presented in this book is based on the author's personal knowledge and understanding of livestock management. The author is not affiliated with any association, company, business, or individual in the livestock industry. All content is provided for informational purposes only and should not be considered as professional advice. Readers are encouraged to seek professional guidance and conduct their own research before making any decisions based on the information contained in this book. The author and publisher disclaim any liability for any adverse effects or consequences resulting from the use of the information contained herein.

Table of Contents

CHAPTER ONE 15

Introduction To Cricket Farming 15

Overview Of Cricket Farming 15

Benefits Of Cricket Farming 17

Basic Requirements 18

    1. Housing: 18

    2. Temperature and Humidity: 19

    3. Food and Water: 19

    4. Cleaning and Maintenance: 19

Common Misconceptions 20

Key Terms And Definitions 21

    1. Enclosure: 21

    2. Brood Stock: 22

    3. Molting: 22

    4. Harvesting: 22

CHAPTER TWO 23

Setting Up Your Cricket Farm 23

Choosing The Right Location 23

Essential Equipment And Supplies 24

    1. Containers and Enclosures: 24

    2. Substrate Material: 25

    3. Food and Water Supply: 25

    4. Temperature and Humidity Control: ...26

Setting Up Enclosures And Habitat 26

Environmental Conditions (Temperature, Humidity, Lighting) 27

Cost Estimates And Budgeting 29

CHAPTER THREE 31

Selecting And Purchasing Crickets 31

Types Of Crickets Suitable For Farming 31

    • House Cricket (Acheta domesticus): 31

- Banded Cricket (Gryllodes sigillatus): ..32
- Field Cricket (Gryllus campestris): 32

Where To Purchase Crickets 33
- Specialized Cricket Breeders: 33
- Online Suppliers: 34
- Local Pet Stores: 34

Understanding Cricket Life Stages 35
- Egg Stage: 35
- Nymph Stage: 35
- Adult Stage: 36

How To Inspect Quality 36
- Health Check: 36
- Activity Level: 37
- Size and Growth: 37
- Environmental Conditions: 37

Initial Stocking Recommendations 38

- Starting Quantity: 38
- Age Distribution: 39
- Habitat Setup: 39
- Monitoring and Adjusting: 39

CHAPTER FOUR 41

Feeding And Nutrition 41

Types Of Feed For Crickets 41

Nutritional Requirements 42

Feeding Schedule And Quantities 44

Supplements And Additives 45

Common Feeding Issues And Solutions 46

CHAPTER FIVE 49

Breeding Crickets 49

Understanding Cricket Reproduction 49

Setting Up Breeding Conditions 50

Managing Breeding Colonies 52

Incubation And Hatchling Care 53

Common Breeding Problems 54

CHAPTER SIX 57

Health And Disease Management 57

Identifying Common Cricket Diseases 57

Preventative Health Measures 58

Treatment Options For Infections 60

Pest Control 62

Monitoring And Record-Keeping 63

CHAPTER SEVEN 65

Harvesting Crickets 65

Timing And Indicators For Harvesting 65

Methods For Collecting Crickets 66

Processing And Packaging 68

Ensuring Quality And Freshness 69

Handling And Storage 70

CHAPTER EIGHT ... 73

Marketing And Selling Crickets ... 73

Identifying Potential Markets ... 73

Pricing Strategies ... 75

Creating A Brand And Marketing Plan ... 76

Distribution Channels ... 77

Legal Considerations And Regulations ... 78

CHAPTER NINE ... 81

Troubleshooting Common Issues ... 81

Common Problems And Solutions ... 81

Diagnosing Environmental Issues ... 83

Managing Unexpected Costs ... 85

Adjusting To Market Fluctuations ... 86

Seeking Expert Advice ... 88

CHAPTER TEN ... 91

Expanding And Scaling Your Farm ... 91

Evaluating Growth Opportunities 91

Upgrading Equipment And Facilities 92

Increasing Production Capacity 94

Diversifying Product Offerings 95

Planning For Long-Term Success 97

Frequently Asked Question And Their Answers
.... 99

CONCLUSION 105

THE END 109

ABOUT THIS BOOK

This book Cricket Farming is an essential guide for anyone interested in this burgeoning field, offering a comprehensive roadmap from initial setup to advanced scaling strategies. The introduction provides a thorough overview of cricket farming, detailing its numerous benefits and outlining the basic requirements for starting. By debunking common misconceptions and clarifying key terms, it sets the stage for a successful venture.

The guide delves into the crucial aspects of setting up a cricket farm, starting with the selection of an optimal location and the acquisition of essential equipment. It covers the specifics of creating suitable enclosures and maintaining the right environmental conditions, including temperature, humidity, and lighting, all while offering practical advice on budgeting and cost management.

When it comes to selecting and purchasing crickets, This book provides valuable insights into choosing the right species, sourcing them from reputable suppliers, and understanding their life stages. It emphasizes the importance of inspecting quality and offers initial stocking recommendations to ensure a strong start.

Feeding and nutrition are pivotal elements of successful cricket farming. This book addresses various feed types, nutritional requirements, and feeding schedules, alongside guidance on supplements and common feeding issues. This ensures that readers can maintain healthy and productive cricket colonies.

The breeding section offers an in-depth look at cricket reproduction, from setting up breeding conditions to managing colonies and caring for hatchlings.

It also addresses common breeding problems, providing practical solutions for overcoming these challenges.

Health and disease management are crucial for maintaining a thriving farm. This book covers common diseases, preventative measures, treatment options, and pest control, with an emphasis on diligent monitoring and record-keeping to ensure overall health.

Harvesting crickets is another key area of focus. The guide explains the timing and indicators for harvesting, methods for collection, processing, and packaging, as well as ensuring quality and freshness in handling and storage.

Marketing and selling crickets are explored in detail, with advice on identifying potential markets, setting pricing strategies, creating a brand, and navigating distribution channels.

It also covers legal considerations and regulations to ensure compliance and success in the marketplace.

The troubleshooting section equips readers with solutions for common problems, from environmental issues to market fluctuations and unexpected costs. It underscores the importance of seeking expert advice when needed.

Finally, This book addresses expanding and scaling a cricket farm. It provides strategies for evaluating growth opportunities, upgrading equipment, increasing production capacity, and diversifying product offerings, all while planning for long-term success in the industry.

CHAPTER ONE

Introduction To Cricket Farming

Overview Of Cricket Farming

Cricket farming involves raising crickets in a controlled environment to harvest them for various uses, including animal feed, human consumption, and bait. This practice, also known as cricket cultivation or entomophagy, is gaining traction due to its sustainability and efficiency compared to traditional livestock farming. Crickets are a rich source of protein, vitamins, and minerals, making them an attractive option for those seeking alternative protein sources.

Cricket farming can be done on a small scale, such as in backyard setups, or on a larger, commercial scale. The farming process generally involves creating an environment that mimics the crickets' natural habitat, including temperature, humidity, and lighting conditions. Farmers must ensure that crickets have access to appropriate food and water sources to thrive. This process can be both rewarding and challenging, requiring attention to detail and a willingness to learn about cricket biology and husbandry.

The basic concept of cricket farming involves setting up a habitat where crickets can grow and reproduce. The habitat typically consists of breeding containers or enclosures equipped with the right environmental controls. The crickets are provided with food and water, and their growth and reproduction are monitored to ensure optimal conditions. Harvesting occurs once the crickets reach maturity, and they are then processed according to their intended use.

Benefits Of Cricket Farming

Cricket farming offers several notable benefits. One of the primary advantages is its environmental impact. Crickets require significantly less land, water, and feed compared to traditional livestock. They produce fewer greenhouse gases and have a lower ecological footprint, making them a more sustainable option for protein production.

In addition to environmental benefits, crickets are highly nutritious. They are rich in protein, contain all essential amino acids, and are also a good source of vitamins and minerals such as B vitamins, iron, and calcium. This nutritional profile makes crickets a valuable food source for both humans and animals.

Cricket farming can also be economically beneficial. The initial setup costs can be relatively low compared to other forms of agriculture, and crickets reproduce quickly, allowing for a rapid turnover.

This efficiency can lead to a profitable venture, especially if there is a market for cricket-based products such as protein powders, snacks, or animal feed.

Basic Requirements

To start cricket farming, several basic requirements must be met to ensure the successful growth and reproduction of the crickets. The primary requirements include:

1. Housing: Crickets need a habitat that provides adequate space, ventilation, and environmental control. This can be achieved with specially designed enclosures or containers that allow for easy management and monitoring. The housing should be secure to prevent escape and protect the crickets from pests or predators.

2. **Temperature and Humidity:** Crickets thrive in specific temperature and humidity ranges. Generally, they require temperatures between 80-90°F (27-32°C) and humidity levels of 50-70%. Maintaining these conditions is crucial for their growth and reproduction.

3. **Food and Water:** Crickets need a balanced diet to grow and reproduce effectively. They can be fed a variety of foods, including commercial cricket feed, vegetables, and grains. Fresh water must be available at all times, as dehydration can affect their health and productivity.

4. **Cleaning and Maintenance:** Regular cleaning of the cricket habitat is essential to prevent the buildup of waste and to reduce the risk of disease. This includes removing dead crickets, cleaning feeding and watering equipment, and ensuring proper ventilation to maintain air quality.

Common Misconceptions

There are several common misconceptions about cricket farming that can deter potential farmers. One misconception is that crickets are difficult to manage or require complex equipment. In reality, cricket farming can be straightforward with the right setup and knowledge. Basic equipment and proper care are usually sufficient to maintain a healthy cricket population.

Another misconception is that crickets are unsanitary or pose health risks. When managed properly, cricket farms can be as clean and safe as any other agricultural operation. Regular cleaning, good hygiene practices, and proper handling procedures help ensure that crickets remain healthy and that any products derived from them are safe for consumption.

Additionally, some people believe that crickets are not a viable source of protein compared to traditional livestock. However, crickets are highly nutritious, offering a comparable or even superior protein profile to other animal proteins. Their efficient feed conversion and lower environmental impact further support their viability as a protein source.

Key Terms And Definitions

Understanding key terms related to cricket farming can help streamline the learning process and facilitate effective communication. Here are some essential terms:

1. **Enclosure:** A controlled environment where crickets are housed and managed. Enclosures can range from small containers to large, climate-controlled rooms, depending on the scale of the operation.

2. **Brood Stock:** The population of crickets used for breeding. Maintaining a healthy and diverse brood stock is essential for successful reproduction and overall farm productivity.

3. **Molting:** The process by which crickets shed their exoskeleton to grow. Crickets go through several molts during their life cycle, and this process is crucial for their development.

4. **Harvesting:** The process of collecting mature crickets for processing or sale. Timing the harvest is important to ensure the optimal size and quality of the crickets.

By familiarizing yourself with these terms and concepts, you can better understand the cricket farming process and effectively manage your cricket farming operation.

CHAPTER TWO

Setting Up Your Cricket Farm

Choosing The Right Location

Selecting the ideal location for your cricket farm is crucial to ensure the success and efficiency of your operation. Begin by choosing a location that is easily accessible but offers some level of isolation from external disturbances. This could be a spare room in your house, a dedicated shed, or a section of a larger barn. The area should be clean and free from pests or contaminants that could affect the health of your crickets.

The location should have adequate space to accommodate all the necessary equipment and provide room for expansion as your farm grows. Ensure that the space can be easily ventilated and is free from extreme temperature fluctuations.

Avoid placing your cricket farm in areas prone to high humidity or direct sunlight, as these conditions can adversely affect cricket's health.

Additionally, consider the proximity to water sources and electricity. Regular access to water is necessary for maintaining proper humidity levels, while electricity will be needed for lighting and heating systems. A location with these amenities readily available will simplify the setup process and ongoing maintenance of your farm.

Essential Equipment And Supplies

To start a cricket farm, you'll need a range of essential equipment and supplies to create a suitable environment for your crickets. The basic items include:

1. Containers and Enclosures: Crickets can be raised in large bins or enclosures made from plastic

or metal. Choose containers with secure lids to prevent escapes and easy-to-clean surfaces to maintain hygiene. Bins should be large enough to accommodate the growing cricket population and allow for movement and breeding.

2. Substrate Material: Provide a substrate for crickets to lay their eggs and for optimal living conditions. Common substrates include crushed eggshells, sand, or specialized cricket bedding. This material helps in absorbing moisture and provides a natural habitat for the crickets.

3. Food and Water Supply: Crickets require a balanced diet to thrive. Invest in high-quality cricket food, which typically includes grains, vegetables, and protein supplements. Additionally, provide a constant source of water, either through shallow dishes or a water gel, to keep the crickets hydrated.

4. Temperature and Humidity Control: Crickets thrive in a controlled environment. Equip your farm with heaters and humidifiers to maintain the ideal temperature and humidity levels. Thermometers and hygrometers will help you monitor these conditions regularly.

Setting Up Enclosures And Habitat

Setting up the enclosures and habitat is a key step in creating a productive cricket farm. Start by cleaning and disinfecting the containers to ensure they are free from contaminants. Next, prepare the substrate by spreading it evenly across the bottom of the enclosure. This substrate should be deep enough to allow crickets to burrow and lay eggs.

Arrange the enclosures in a way that allows for easy access and maintenance. Place food and water sources within each container, ensuring they are accessible to all crickets.

Additionally, provide hiding spots using cardboard tubes or egg cartons, as crickets need shelter to feel secure and reduce stress.

For optimal breeding, introduce a few breeding pairs of crickets to each enclosure. Crickets prefer to lay eggs in a dark and moist environment, so ensure that the substrate remains damp but not soggy. Regularly check the enclosures for signs of mold or decay and remove any uneaten food or waste to maintain a clean environment.

Environmental Conditions (Temperature, Humidity, Lighting)

Crickets require specific environmental conditions to thrive. The ideal temperature for crickets is between 80-90°F (27-32°C). Use heaters or heating pads to maintain this temperature range, especially in colder climates. Temperature fluctuations can stress the crickets and impact their growth and reproduction.

Humidity is equally important. Maintain a humidity level of around 50-70% to ensure that the crickets remain hydrated and their habitat stays conducive to breeding. Use a hygrometer to monitor humidity levels and employ humidifiers or moisture-retentive substrates to regulate them.

Lighting should be carefully managed to mimic natural day-night cycles. Provide 12-14 hours of light followed by 10-12 hours of darkness each day. This helps regulate cricket activity and reproductive cycles. Use fluorescent or LED lights that are energy-efficient and generate minimal heat to avoid overheating the enclosure.

Cost Estimates And Budgeting

Understanding the cost estimates and budgeting for your cricket farm will help you manage your expenses and plan for future growth. Initial costs include purchasing equipment, such as enclosures, heaters, humidifiers, and lighting. Estimate these costs based on the size of your operation and the quality of the equipment.

Ongoing expenses include food, water, electricity for temperature and humidity control, and maintenance supplies. Budget for regular purchases of cricket food and substrate materials, as well as any potential repairs or upgrades to your equipment.

Consider the potential revenue from selling crickets to offset your costs. Research market prices for crickets and calculate your expected income based on your production capacity. Creating a detailed budget and financial plan will help you track your expenses and ensure the sustainability of your cricket farm.

CHAPTER THREE

Selecting And Purchasing Crickets

Types Of Crickets Suitable For Farming

When starting a cricket farming venture, selecting the right species is crucial. The most commonly farmed crickets are the House Cricket (Acheta domesticus), Banded Cricket (Gryllodes sigillatus), and Field Cricket (Gryllus campestris). Each species has its own set of advantages and considerations, making it essential to choose one that aligns with your farming goals.

- **House Cricket (Acheta domesticus):** This species is the most popular for commercial farming due to its high reproductive rate and adaptability to various environments.

House crickets thrive in indoor environments and can be bred year-round, which makes them ideal for consistent production. They are also known for their protein-rich bodies, making them valuable for animal feed and human consumption.

- Banded Cricket (Gryllodes sigillatus): Banded crickets are smaller than house crickets but are known for their hardiness and resistance to diseases. They are well-suited for farming in conditions with slight variations in temperature and humidity. They also exhibit a slower growth rate compared to house crickets, which may be advantageous for some farmers looking to manage their production cycle more carefully.

- Field Cricket (Gryllus campestris): These crickets are larger and robust, ideal for outdoor farming systems. They can handle a wider range of temperatures and conditions but require more space compared to a house or banded crickets. Their larger size makes them suitable for specific markets, such as pet food or live bait.

Understanding the characteristics and requirements of these cricket species will help you make an informed decision about which type is best suited for your farming setup.

Where To Purchase Crickets

Purchasing crickets from reliable sources is vital to ensure the health and quality of your initial stock. Here are some options for acquiring crickets:

• **Specialized Cricket Breeders:** Many cricket farms and breeders offer high-quality, disease-free crickets. They often provide a variety of species and age groups, allowing you to choose the best fit for your farming needs. Look for breeders with a good reputation and positive reviews to ensure you receive healthy crickets.

· **Online Suppliers:** Numerous online platforms and suppliers specialize in crickets and other live feed products. These suppliers often have a wide selection and can ship directly to your location. When purchasing online, verify the supplier's credibility and check for customer feedback to ensure the quality of the crickets.

· **Local Pet Stores:** Some pet stores carry live crickets, especially those catering to reptile owners. While these crickets can be a convenient option, they may not always be the best choice for large-scale farming due to limited availability and higher costs. Ensure the crickets are fresh and healthy before purchasing.

When buying crickets, it's essential to ask about their origin, health status, and any treatments they may have received. This information will help you avoid introducing pests or diseases into your cricket farm.

Understanding Cricket Life Stages

Crickets undergo several life stages, each with different care requirements and characteristics. Familiarizing yourself with these stages will help you manage your cricket population effectively:

- **Egg Stage:** Crickets lay eggs in small clusters or pods. The eggs are delicate and require specific humidity and temperature conditions to hatch successfully. During this stage, it's important to maintain optimal environmental conditions to ensure high hatching rates.

- **Nymph Stage:** After hatching, crickets enter the nymph stage. Nymphs resemble small adults but lack fully developed wings and reproductive organs. They molt several times before reaching maturity. Providing adequate food, water, and space during this stage is crucial for healthy growth.

- Adult Stage: Adult crickets are fully developed and capable of reproduction. They require a well-balanced diet and appropriate conditions to maintain their health and productivity. Monitoring the population density and ensuring proper ventilation are essential to prevent overcrowding and disease.

Understanding these stages helps in planning your cricket farming operations, including breeding schedules, habitat management, and harvesting.

How To Inspect Quality

Ensuring the quality of crickets before purchasing is essential for a successful farming venture. Here's how to inspect crickets for quality:

- Health Check: Examine the crickets for signs of disease or pests. Healthy crickets should have clean, intact bodies with no visible injuries or abnormalities. Check for signs of fungal infections, mites, or other parasites that could impact their well-being.

- Activity Level: Healthy crickets are generally active and responsive. They should exhibit normal behaviors such as hopping and exploring their environment. Avoid crickets that are lethargic or show signs of weakness.

- Size and Growth: Evaluate the size and growth stage of the crickets. Consistent size and development indicate a well-maintained breeding environment. Avoid purchasing crickets that appear underdeveloped or stunted, as they may have been poorly cared for or subjected to adverse conditions.

- Environmental Conditions: Assess the conditions in which the crickets are kept. Ensure that the breeding environment is clean and well-maintained, with proper temperature and humidity controls. This can provide insight into the overall health and quality of the crickets.

By carefully inspecting the crickets before purchase, you can minimize the risk of introducing unhealthy or poorly managed stock into your farming setup.

Initial Stocking Recommendations

When starting your cricket farm, stocking the right quantity and size of crickets is key to a successful operation. Here are some recommendations for initial stocking:

· **Starting Quantity:** Begin with a manageable number of crickets to ensure you can provide adequate care and monitor their development effectively. A common starting point for beginners is 1,000 to 2,000 crickets, which allows you to gauge their growth and adjust your management practices as needed.

- **Age Distribution:** Stocking a mix of nymphs and adults can help establish a stable breeding population. Having nymphs will ensure a continuous supply of crickets as they grow into adults and reproduce. Ensure you have enough adult crickets to initiate breeding and maintain a sustainable population.

- **Habitat Setup:** Provide an appropriate habitat for your crickets, including nesting areas, food sources, and water. Proper habitat setup is crucial for the health and productivity of your crickets. Ensure the enclosure is well-ventilated and easy to clean to maintain optimal conditions.

- **Monitoring and Adjusting:** Regularly monitor your cricket population and adjust stocking levels as needed based on growth rates and reproduction. Keeping detailed records of your cricket numbers, health, and production will help you make informed decisions and optimize your farming practices.

Following these stocking recommendations will help establish a strong foundation for your cricket farm, leading to a more successful and sustainable operation.

CHAPTER FOUR

Feeding And Nutrition

Types Of Feed For Crickets

Crickets require a balanced diet to thrive, and understanding the types of feed available is essential for maintaining their health. The primary types of feed include commercial cricket food, grains, vegetables, and protein sources. Commercial cricket foods are specially formulated to meet the nutritional needs of crickets and typically contain a blend of grains, protein, vitamins, and minerals. These feeds are convenient as they are ready to use and ensure a balanced diet for your crickets.

In addition to commercial feeds, you can also provide crickets with grains such as oats, wheat bran, and cornmeal.

These grains are excellent sources of carbohydrates and fiber, which are important for digestion and overall health. Fresh vegetables, like carrots, potatoes, and leafy greens, can also be included in their diet to provide essential vitamins and minerals. Protein sources like fish flakes, chicken feed, or powdered eggs can be added to enhance their growth and reproduction.

When choosing feed, it's crucial to select options that are free of mold and contaminants. Moldy feed can lead to respiratory issues and other health problems in crickets. Additionally, ensure that the feed is appropriate for the cricket species you are raising, as different species might have slightly different dietary needs.

Nutritional Requirements

Crickets have specific nutritional requirements that must be met to ensure optimal health and productivity.

Their diet should include a balance of carbohydrates, proteins, fats, vitamins, and minerals. Carbohydrates, found in grains and vegetables, provide energy for daily activities and growth. Proteins are essential for muscle development and reproduction, making them crucial in the cricket diet.

Fats are also important but should be provided in moderation. They support energy storage and hormone production. Vitamins and minerals play a role in various bodily functions, including immune system support and bone health. Common vitamins required by crickets include Vitamin A, D, and B-complex vitamins. Minerals such as calcium and phosphorus are vital for strong exoskeletons and overall vitality.

To meet these nutritional needs, consider using commercially available cricket food that is nutritionally complete or supplementing their diet with a variety of natural food sources.

Regularly monitor the health of your crickets to ensure they are receiving all the nutrients they need.

Feeding Schedule And Quantities

Establishing a proper feeding schedule is crucial for maintaining healthy crickets. Crickets should be fed daily to ensure they receive a consistent supply of nutrients. The amount of feed depends on the size of the cricket population and their growth stage. For small colonies, you might need to provide a few tablespoons of feed per day, while larger colonies will require more.

Observe your crickets to gauge their consumption and adjust the quantities accordingly. Avoid overfeeding, as uneaten food can spoil and create unsanitary conditions in the habitat. Generally, crickets will eat about 10-15% of their body weight in food per day.

Ensure that fresh food is available and remove any uneaten portions to prevent mold and bacterial growth.

During different stages of their life cycle—such as nymphs, juveniles, and adults—the feeding requirements might change. Nymphs and juveniles typically require more protein for growth, while adults may need a more balanced diet to support reproduction and energy needs.

Supplements And Additives

Supplements and additives can enhance the nutritional value of the crickets' diet and address specific health needs. Calcium supplements are particularly important, especially for breeding females, to support eggshell development and overall health. You can use commercially available calcium powders or crush calcium-rich foods like eggshells and add them to their feed.

Vitamin supplements can also be beneficial, particularly if you are using a diet that lacks certain vitamins. Multivitamin powders or liquid supplements can be mixed into the feed to ensure that crickets receive a well-rounded nutrient profile.

Occasionally, crickets may benefit from probiotics to promote healthy gut flora, especially if they are showing signs of digestive issues. Probiotic powders or supplements can be added to their feed to improve digestion and overall health.

Common Feeding Issues And Solutions

Feeding crickets can come with a few common issues that need to be addressed to maintain a healthy colony. One issue is the growth of mold or bacteria on uneaten food, which can cause respiratory problems and other health issues.

To prevent this, regularly clean the feeding area and remove any leftover food promptly.

Another issue is overfeeding or underfeeding. Overfeeding can lead to waste and unsanitary conditions, while underfeeding can result in malnutrition and poor growth. Monitor the cricket population and adjust feeding quantities as needed. Ensure that crickets have constant access to fresh food and water.

If crickets appear lethargic or are not eating, it may indicate a problem with their diet or habitat conditions. Check the quality of the food, the cleanliness of the environment, and the overall health of the crickets. Sometimes, adjusting the diet or improving habitat conditions can resolve these issues.

By understanding and managing these aspects of feeding and nutrition, you can ensure that your crickets remain healthy and productive, making cricket farming a successful venture.

CHAPTER FIVE

Breeding Crickets

Understanding Cricket Reproduction

Cricket reproduction involves understanding the basic biology and behavior of crickets to ensure successful breeding. Crickets are oviparous, meaning they lay eggs that develop outside the mother's body. The reproductive process begins with mating, where the male cricket produces a mating call to attract females. Once a female selects a mate, copulation occurs, and the female lays eggs on a suitable substrate.

Crickets have specific mating behaviors and require optimal environmental conditions to reproduce effectively.

Females lay eggs in a damp, dark, and warm environment, often using a specialized ovipositor to deposit eggs into the soil or a similar medium. Each female can lay hundreds of eggs, which eventually hatch into nymphs. Understanding these stages is crucial for managing successful cricket breeding.

To optimize cricket reproduction, ensure that you provide an environment that mimics their natural habitat. This includes maintaining appropriate temperature, humidity, and light cycles. Proper care during each reproductive stage will increase the likelihood of successful egg development and hatching.

Setting Up Breeding Conditions

Creating the ideal breeding environment for crickets involves replicating their natural habitat as closely as possible. Start by setting up a breeding enclosure with the appropriate substrate for egg-laying.

A mixture of soil and sand or commercial egg-laying trays works well. Ensure the substrate is moist but not waterlogged, as this can affect egg viability.

Temperature plays a crucial role in cricket breeding. Maintain a consistent temperature of around 80-85°F (27-29°C), which is optimal for reproduction. Use a heat lamp or heat mat to regulate the temperature, and avoid sudden fluctuations. Humidity is also essential; keep the humidity level between 50-70% to ensure the eggs do not dry out.

Light cycles are important for regulating cricket activity. Provide a 12-hour light and 12-hour dark cycle to simulate natural conditions. This helps maintain the crickets' natural rhythms and promotes healthy reproductive behavior. Regularly clean the breeding enclosure to prevent mold and bacteria growth, which can adversely affect both adult crickets and eggs.

Managing Breeding Colonies

Managing a breeding colony involves monitoring and maintaining the health and productivity of both adult crickets and their offspring. Start by ensuring that the colony has a balanced ratio of males to females. Too many males can lead to aggressive behavior, while too few females can reduce egg production. A good ratio is about 1 male to 2-3 females.

Regularly check the breeding enclosure for signs of overcrowding. Crickets need space to move around and lay eggs comfortably. Overcrowding can lead to stress and increased mortality rates. Provide ample food and water, and offer a variety of food sources such as grains, vegetables, and fruit. This ensures that crickets receive a balanced diet, which is crucial for their health and reproductive success.

Monitor the health of your crickets by checking for signs of disease or abnormal behavior. Remove any dead or sick crickets promptly to prevent the spread of illness. Maintain clean conditions in the enclosure to reduce the risk of disease. Regularly inspect the substrate for eggs and replace it as needed to ensure a continuous supply of healthy hatchlings.

Incubation And Hatchling Care

Once eggs are laid, the incubation period begins. Crickets' eggs typically hatch within 1-2 weeks, depending on temperature and humidity. Maintain the incubation environment by keeping the substrate moist and at the proper temperature. Avoid disturbing the eggs to prevent damage.

After hatching, you'll need to provide care for the nymphs, which are small and vulnerable. Transfer them to a separate enclosure with fine mesh to prevent escape.

Offer finely ground food and water, ensuring that it is easily accessible to the tiny nymphs. As they grow, gradually introduce larger food items and increase the size of their enclosure to accommodate their growth.

Regularly clean the nymph enclosure to prevent the buildup of waste and mold. Provide hiding spots and substrate to allow the nymphs to feel secure. Monitor their development closely, as proper care during this stage is critical for their transition into healthy adults.

Common Breeding Problems

Several common issues can arise during cricket breeding, and understanding how to address them can ensure a successful operation. One common problem is insufficient egg production, often caused by inadequate environmental conditions or an imbalanced male-to-female ratio.

Ensure that the breeding environment is optimal and adjust the ratio if needed.

Another issue is the development of mold or bacteria in the breeding enclosure, which can harm both eggs and crickets. Regular cleaning and maintaining proper humidity levels can prevent this. If mold appears, replace the substrate and clean the enclosure thoroughly.

Crickets can also suffer from overcrowding, leading to stress and increased mortality rates. Provide adequate space and resources to prevent this. If you notice signs of overcrowding, consider expanding the enclosure or separating the crickets into multiple breeding setups.

Regular monitoring and addressing these common problems proactively will help maintain a healthy and productive cricket breeding operation.

CHAPTER SIX

Health And Disease Management

Identifying Common Cricket Diseases

Crickets, like any other livestock, are susceptible to various diseases that can affect their health and productivity. One of the most common diseases in cricket farming is fungal infections. These infections are often caused by improper humidity levels and poor ventilation in the cricket habitat. Symptoms include a white, powdery substance on the cricket's body or within the habitat, which is indicative of fungal growth. Another common issue is bacterial infections, which can manifest as swollen limbs or abnormal body discoloration. Bacterial infections are usually linked to unsanitary conditions and can spread rapidly if not addressed.

Viral diseases can also affect crickets, although they are less common than fungal or bacterial issues. Symptoms might include sudden death without any visible signs of illness, or a noticeable drop in activity and feeding. Crickets with viral infections often show no external symptoms until it is too late. It's crucial for cricket farmers to regularly inspect their crickets and their habitat to catch these diseases early. Parasitic infections are another concern, where parasites like mites or worms can infest crickets, leading to reduced health and growth. Regular checks for unusual behavior or physical abnormalities are essential in identifying these infestations.

Preventative Health Measures

Preventative health measures are critical in maintaining a healthy cricket population and preventing the outbreak of diseases.

One of the primary measures is maintaining optimal environmental conditions. Crickets thrive in a controlled environment with specific temperature and humidity levels. Keeping the habitat at the recommended temperature of 80-85°F (27-29°C) and humidity of 50-60% helps prevent many health issues. Additionally, proper ventilation ensures that excess moisture does not accumulate, which can lead to fungal growth and other health problems.

Hygiene and sanitation play a significant role in disease prevention. Regular cleaning of cricket containers and removal of uneaten food reduces the risk of bacterial and fungal infections. Implementing a disinfection protocol using safe, non-toxic cleaners will help keep the environment free from pathogens. Additionally, ensuring that crickets have access to clean water and high-quality food supplements their immune system, making them less susceptible to diseases.

Another effective preventive measure is quarantine procedures. Introducing new crickets into the existing population without proper quarantine can introduce new diseases. It is advisable to isolate new arrivals for a few weeks and monitor their health before mixing them with the main colony. This practice helps to ensure that any potential diseases are caught early and do not spread throughout the entire population.

Treatment Options For Infections

When crickets fall ill, prompt and effective treatment is necessary to manage infections and prevent further spread. For fungal infections, applying antifungal treatments directly to the affected areas or within the habitat can help manage the disease. Commercial antifungal sprays or powders designed for insect use can be effective.

Ensure that the habitat is well-ventilated and humidity levels are adjusted to prevent the recurrence of fungal issues.

In the case of bacterial infections, the treatment often involves improving sanitation and using antibacterial agents. Removing contaminated substrates and thoroughly cleaning the habitat is essential. For individual crickets showing signs of bacterial infection, using an appropriate antibacterial solution can help. Consult with a veterinarian for the right type of medication and dosage, especially for larger colonies where a systemic treatment might be necessary.

Parasitic infections require specific treatments depending on the type of parasite. For mites, using mite sprays or powders that are safe for crickets can help eliminate the parasites. If worms are the issue, a suitable dewormer may be required. It is important to follow the instructions carefully and consider consulting with a specialist to ensure the chosen treatment is effective and safe for the crickets.

Pest Control

Effective pest control is essential to protect crickets from pests that can harm their health and productivity. Regular inspections of the cricket habitat are crucial to identifying and addressing pest issues early. Common pests include mites, flies, and beetles. Mites, for example, can be controlled using commercial mite sprays or powders specifically designed for insects. Ensure that any treatment used is safe for crickets and applied according to the manufacturer's instructions.

Implementing physical barriers can also help in controlling pests. For instance, using fine mesh screens on ventilation openings can prevent flies and beetles from entering the cricket habitat. Additionally, traps can be strategically placed to monitor and reduce pest populations. Regular cleaning and maintenance of the habitat reduce attractants such as food waste that might lure pests.

Natural predators can also play a role in pest control. Introducing beneficial insects that prey on common cricket pests can help keep the population in check. However, this method requires careful management to ensure that the introduced predators do not harm the crickets themselves. Always research and choose predators that are compatible with your cricket farming system.

Monitoring And Record-Keeping

Effective monitoring and record-keeping are vital for maintaining the health and productivity of a cricket farm. Regular health checks should be conducted to identify any signs of disease or distress among the crickets. Observing changes in behavior, feeding patterns, and overall health can provide early indicators of potential issues. Keeping detailed records of these observations helps track health trends and identify recurring problems.

Maintaining environmental records is also important. Documenting temperature, humidity, and cleanliness levels can help ensure that the habitat conditions remain within the optimal range. This data can be invaluable in diagnosing problems and adjusting conditions to prevent health issues.

Treatment and intervention records should be kept meticulously. Recording details of any treatments administered, including the type of treatment, dosage, and dates, help in evaluating their effectiveness and planning future interventions. This also provides a historical record that can be useful for troubleshooting and improving management practices.

CHAPTER SEVEN

Harvesting Crickets

Timing And Indicators For Harvesting

The timing of cricket harvesting is crucial for maximizing yield and quality. Generally, crickets are ready for harvest about 6-8 weeks after hatching. This period allows them to grow to a size suitable for consumption or sale. Observing the crickets' growth stages can help determine the best harvest time.

Indicators that crickets are ready for harvesting include their size and coloration. Adult crickets, known as "adults," are usually the most suitable for harvest, as they have reached their full size. Look for crickets that are approximately 1-2 inches in length. They should have a firm, glossy exoskeleton. Additionally, crickets that are starting to exhibit signs of molting or are no longer as active are nearing the end of their life cycle and should be harvested promptly to prevent loss.

Another indicator is the density of the cricket population. If the enclosure appears overcrowded and crickets are beginning to fight or show signs of stress, it's time to harvest. Proper timing ensures that the crickets are harvested at their peak and minimizes the risk of diseases or cannibalism.

Methods For Collecting Crickets

Collecting crickets requires a systematic approach to ensure efficiency and minimize stress for the insects. One effective method is using a vacuum collection system, which gently sucks up the crickets into a collection chamber. This system helps in quickly gathering large numbers of crickets with minimal handling. Ensure the vacuum's suction is adjustable to prevent harming the crickets.

Alternatively, manual collection can be done using a mesh scoop or net. Gently sweep the net through the cricket habitat to gather them. This method is more labor-intensive but can be suitable for smaller operations. When using manual methods, handle the crickets carefully to avoid injury and stress. Place them in containers with proper ventilation to ensure they remain alive and healthy until further processing.

Using attractants like light or food can help gather crickets in a specific area, making collection easier. Light traps are particularly useful at night when crickets are more active. Ensure that the collection area is clean and free from contaminants to maintain the quality of the crickets.

Processing And Packaging

After collection, crickets must be processed to ensure they are safe for consumption or sale. Begin by removing any debris or waste from the crickets. A common method is to rinse them gently with clean water, ensuring that any excrement or substrate is removed. After rinsing, place the crickets on a clean, dry surface to allow them to dry completely.

Processing also involves cooking or freezing the crickets, depending on the end use. For consumption, crickets are often roasted or baked to enhance their flavor and texture. Roasting can be done in an oven at around 350°F (175°C) for 10-15 minutes. Ensure that they are evenly roasted to avoid overcooking or burning.

Packaging should be done in a clean environment to avoid contamination. Use airtight containers or vacuum-sealed bags to keep the crickets fresh.

Label the packages with the date of processing and any relevant information. Store the packaged crickets in a cool, dry place or refrigerate them if necessary to extend shelf life.

Ensuring Quality And Freshness

Maintaining the quality and freshness of crickets is vital for consumer satisfaction and marketability. Start by ensuring that the crickets are processed and packaged as soon as possible after harvesting to maintain their freshness. Avoid exposing the crickets to direct sunlight or high temperatures, as this can affect their quality.

Quality control measures should include checking for any signs of spoilage or contamination before packaging. Crickets should have a clean, fresh smell and a crisp texture. Any discolored or malformed crickets should be discarded to ensure only high-quality products reach consumers.

Regularly inspect your cricket farming environment to prevent issues such as mold, bacteria, or pests. Proper hygiene practices, such as cleaning the habitat and equipment regularly, are essential for maintaining the health of your crickets. This proactive approach helps ensure that your crickets remain fresh and of high quality.

Handling And Storage

Proper handling and storage of crickets are critical to maintaining their quality and extending their shelf life. After processing, crickets should be handled with care to avoid damaging them. Use clean gloves and equipment to prevent contamination. Minimize direct handling and avoid unnecessary agitation.

For short-term storage, keep processed crickets in a cool, dry environment. Airtight containers or vacuum-sealed bags are ideal for preventing moisture and air from affecting the crickets.

Ensure that storage areas are well-ventilated to prevent any buildup of humidity.

For long-term storage, consider freezing crickets to extend their shelf life. Freezing should be done as soon as possible after processing. Use freezer-safe bags or containers to protect the crickets from freezer burn. Label and date the containers to track storage duration. When thawing, do so gradually to maintain the quality of the crickets.

By following these procedures, you can efficiently harvest, process, and store crickets, ensuring a high-quality product for your consumers or personal use.

CHAPTER EIGHT

Marketing And Selling Crickets

Identifying Potential Markets

Cricket farming has gained popularity as a sustainable and nutritious alternative protein source. To successfully market and sell crickets, it's crucial to identify potential markets where there is a demand for this product. The first step in identifying potential markets is to research consumer interest and demand. This involves analyzing market trends, consumer preferences, and existing competition in your region. Research can be done through online surveys, focus groups, and industry reports.

Target markets for cricket products include health-conscious consumers, fitness enthusiasts, and those interested in sustainable living.

Crickets are high in protein, vitamins, and minerals, making them appealing to those looking to improve their diet. Additionally, eco-friendly consumers who are conscious of their environmental impact may be interested in crickets as a sustainable protein source. Identify and connect with potential buyers such as health food stores, restaurants, and online marketplaces that focus on specialty or health foods.

Another approach to identifying potential markets is to attend industry events and trade shows. These events provide opportunities to network with industry professionals, learn about market trends, and identify potential customers. Joining relevant industry associations and online forums can also help in understanding the market landscape and connecting with potential buyers.

Pricing Strategies

Pricing your cricket products effectively is essential for profitability and competitiveness. Start by analyzing the costs associated with cricket farming, including feed, equipment, labor, and packaging. Understanding your production costs will help you set a price that covers expenses and generates a profit.

One common pricing strategy is cost-plus pricing, where you add a markup to the cost of production to determine the selling price. This ensures that all costs are covered, and you make a profit. For example, if the cost of producing 100 grams of crickets is $5, and you add a 50% markup, the selling price would be $7.50.

Competitive pricing is another strategy to consider. Research the prices of similar cricket products in the market to determine a competitive price point.

Ensure that your pricing reflects the quality and benefits of your product while remaining attractive to potential buyers. Special promotions, discounts, and bulk pricing can also be used to attract customers and encourage larger purchases.

Creating A Brand And Marketing Plan

Creating a strong brand and marketing plan is essential for differentiating your cricket products from competitors and attracting customers. Start by defining your brand's unique selling points (USPs). What makes your crickets special? It could be their nutritional value, sustainable farming practices, or superior taste. Clearly articulate these USPs in your branding efforts.

Design a professional and appealing logo, packaging, and marketing materials that reflect your brand's identity.

Your branding should communicate the quality and benefits of your cricket products and resonate with your target market. Invest in high-quality packaging that protects the product and enhances its appeal on the shelf.

Develop a comprehensive marketing plan that includes both online and offline strategies. Utilize social media platforms, such as Instagram, Facebook, and Twitter, to reach your target audience and share content about your cricket products. Create a website with detailed information about your products, including their benefits and purchasing options. Additionally, consider collaborating with influencers and bloggers in the health and sustainability niches to promote your products.

Distribution Channels

Effective distribution is crucial for reaching your target market and ensuring that your cricket products are readily available.

Begin by identifying the most suitable distribution channels for your products. Options include direct sales through your website, local health food stores, farmers' markets, and specialty food retailers.

For local distribution, establish relationships with health food stores, grocery stores, and restaurants interested in offering cricket products. Provide samples and promotional materials to potential buyers to showcase the quality of your products. Participating in local farmers' markets and food fairs can also help build brand awareness and attract customers.

Legal Considerations And Regulations

Understanding and complying with legal considerations and regulations is essential for operating a successful cricket farming business. Start by researching local, regional, and national regulations related to food safety and animal husbandry. Regulations may vary depending on your location, so it's important to be aware of the specific requirements in your area.

Ensure that your cricket farming practices comply with food safety standards, including hygiene and sanitation practices. Obtain any necessary permits or licenses required for farming and selling crickets. This may include health department approvals or business licenses.

Labeling requirements are another important aspect. Your product labels should accurately reflect the contents, nutritional information, and any allergens. Compliance with labeling regulations helps ensure transparency and builds trust with your customers.

Additionally, stay informed about any changes in regulations related to the sale of insect-based products.

CHAPTER NINE

Troubleshooting Common Issues

Common Problems And Solutions

Cricket farming, though a rewarding venture, comes with its own set of challenges. One of the most common problems farmers encounter is maintaining the right environmental conditions for cricket growth. Crickets require specific temperature, humidity, and lighting conditions to thrive. If the conditions deviate from the optimal range, crickets can become stressed, leading to reduced growth rates and higher mortality rates. The solution to this problem is to invest in reliable climate control systems. Use thermostats and humidifiers to maintain the environment within the ideal range—typically between 80-90°F (27-32°C) and 50-70%

humidity. Regular monitoring and adjustment are crucial to ensure consistent conditions.

Another issue farmers might face is pest infestations, which can affect the health of crickets. Mites and other small pests can quickly become a problem if not managed properly. Implementing good hygiene practices is key to preventing infestations. Keep the cricket habitat clean and remove any uneaten food promptly. Use pest control methods that are safe for crickets, such as diatomaceous earth, which can help to control mites without harming the crickets. Regular inspections can help identify early signs of pest problems, allowing for timely intervention.

Additionally, cricket farmers may experience issues with cricket nutrition. Providing a balanced diet is essential for healthy growth and reproduction. If crickets are not receiving the necessary nutrients, their growth can be stunted, and reproduction rates can decline.

To address this, ensure that the cricket feed is high-quality and contains a mix of proteins, vitamins, and minerals. Supplement their diet with fresh fruits and vegetables, which can provide additional nutrients. Regularly check the nutritional content of the feed and adjust as necessary to meet the needs of the crickets.

Diagnosing Environmental Issues

Diagnosing environmental issues involves a systematic approach to identify and correct any factors that might be affecting the crickets' health. Start by measuring the temperature and humidity levels in the cricket habitat using reliable instruments. The ideal temperature for crickets is usually between 80-90°F (27-32°C), and the humidity should be maintained at 50-70%. If the measurements are outside these ranges, adjust the heating or cooling systems and the humidifiers or dehumidifiers accordingly.

Another important aspect to check is the ventilation in the cricket habitat. Poor ventilation can lead to stagnant air and increased humidity, which can contribute to the growth of harmful mold and bacteria. Ensure that the habitat has adequate airflow and that any ventilation systems are functioning properly. Clean any air filters regularly to prevent blockages that could affect air quality.

If the crickets are showing signs of stress or disease, such as lethargy or unusual behavior, it's essential to investigate further. Look for signs of mold or mildew, which could indicate high humidity levels, and address any sources of excess moisture. Additionally, inspect the habitat for any potential sources of contamination or stress, such as overcrowding or inadequate food supply.

By systematically addressing these factors, you can maintain a healthy environment for your crickets.

Managing Unexpected Costs

Unexpected costs are a common challenge in cricket farming and can arise from various sources, such as equipment failures, increased feed prices, or necessary repairs. To manage these costs, it's important to have a financial plan and a contingency budget in place. Set aside a portion of your budget specifically for unforeseen expenses, so you have funds readily available when needed.

One way to mitigate unexpected costs is to invest in high-quality, durable equipment that has a longer lifespan. While the initial investment may be higher, it can save you money in the long run by reducing the frequency of repairs and replacements. Additionally, regularly maintain and inspect your equipment to prevent issues before they become major problems. This proactive approach can help minimize downtime and repair costs.

Another strategy is to establish relationships with multiple suppliers for your cricket feed and other essential materials. This can help you negotiate better prices and ensure you have alternatives if prices rise unexpectedly. Keep an eye on market trends and be prepared to adjust your purchasing strategies based on changes in feed costs or other expenses.

Adjusting To Market Fluctuations

Market fluctuations can impact the profitability of cricket farming, especially if the demand for crickets changes or if prices for cricket products vary. To adjust to these fluctuations, it's important to stay informed about market trends and be flexible in your business approach. Monitor the demand for crickets and adjust your production levels accordingly.

If demand decreases, consider scaling back production to avoid surplus and potential financial losses.

Diversifying your product offerings can also help mitigate the effects of market fluctuations. In addition to selling live crickets, you might explore opportunities to sell cricket-based products, such as cricket powder or cricket-based snacks. This diversification can provide additional revenue streams and reduce reliance on a single market.

Finally, establish a network of contacts within the industry, including other cricket farmers and buyers. Building strong relationships can provide valuable insights into market trends and help you make informed decisions about pricing and production. Staying connected with industry professionals can also offer opportunities for collaboration and support during periods of market uncertainty.

Seeking Expert Advice

Seeking expert advice can be a valuable resource in overcoming challenges and improving your cricket farming operations. Experts in the field can provide insights into best practices, help diagnose issues, and offer solutions tailored to your specific situation. Look for professionals with experience in cricket farming or related fields, such as entomology or agriculture.

One way to find expert advice is to join industry associations or groups focused on cricket farming. These organizations often have resources, training programs, and networking opportunities that can connect you with experienced professionals. Attending conferences, workshops, or webinars can also provide access to valuable information and expertise.

In addition to formal sources of advice, consider reaching out to other cricket farmers who have faced similar challenges. Networking with peers can offer practical tips and solutions based on real-world experience. Don't hesitate to ask questions and seek guidance when needed, as leveraging the knowledge of experts and experienced farmers can help you navigate the complexities of cricket farming more effectively.

CHAPTER TEN

Expanding And Scaling Your Farm

Evaluating Growth Opportunities

Expanding your cricket farm begins with evaluating growth opportunities. This involves analyzing current operations and identifying areas with potential for improvement. Start by assessing your farm's performance metrics, such as production rates, operational costs, and profit margins. Look for trends in your data that indicate growth potential, such as increasing demand for your crickets or improved feed conversion rates.

Next, consider market demand. Research local and international markets to understand where opportunities for expansion lie. Identify potential buyers, such as pet food companies, bait shops, or even direct consumers interested in cricket-based products. Evaluate their needs and preferences to determine if you can meet them with your current setup or if modifications are necessary.

Finally, conduct a SWOT analysis (Strengths, Weaknesses, Opportunities, Threats) for your cricket farm. This helps pinpoint internal factors that could support growth, such as efficient production processes or established customer relationships, as well as external factors like competitive advantages or market gaps. Use this analysis to develop a strategic plan that outlines clear objectives and actionable steps for scaling your operations.

Upgrading Equipment And Facilities

Upgrading equipment and facilities is crucial for scaling your cricket farm efficiently. Start by evaluating your current setup and identifying outdated or inefficient equipment. For instance, if your current breeding containers are small and not optimized for cricket growth, consider investing in larger, more advanced containers that offer better climate control and space utilization.

Invest in automated systems where possible. Automated feeders, water dispensers, and climate control systems can significantly reduce labor costs and improve production efficiency. For instance, a well-designed climate control system will maintain optimal temperature and humidity levels, ensuring healthy cricket growth and consistent production.

Additionally, improve your processing and packaging facilities. As your production volume increases, you'll need to handle larger quantities of crickets. Upgrading to industrial-grade processing equipment and efficient packaging solutions will streamline your operations and maintain product quality. Regular maintenance and periodic upgrades are essential to keep your equipment in top condition and avoid costly breakdowns.

Increasing Production Capacity

To increase production capacity, start by optimizing your current processes. Assess your breeding cycles and identify any bottlenecks. For example, if your breeding rooms are overcrowded or if you experience high mortality rates, it might be time to redesign your space or improve breeding conditions.

Consider scaling up your infrastructure. If you're using small containers for breeding, you might need to switch to larger units or multiple racks to accommodate a higher volume of crickets. Ensure that your new setup includes efficient waste management systems to handle the increased production load.

Implementing a phased expansion plan is also effective. Start by incrementally increasing the number of breeding units or growing areas, monitoring the results, and adjusting as needed. This approach minimizes risks and allows you to refine your processes before committing to a larger-scale expansion. Track performance metrics closely to ensure that your capacity increases align with your production goals.

Diversifying Product Offerings

Diversifying your product offerings is a key strategy for expanding your cricket farm's market reach and profitability. Begin by exploring different uses for crickets beyond live insects. Consider processing crickets into powder for protein supplements, creating cricket-based snacks, or developing other value-added products.

Research potential markets for these products. For example, cricket powder is popular in health foods and supplements due to its high protein content. Pet food companies might be interested in cricket-based ingredients for pet nutrition. Assess the feasibility of producing these products by evaluating the required equipment, production processes, and regulatory requirements.

Once you've identified new product opportunities, develop a business plan that includes market analysis, production costs, and pricing strategies. Pilot-test your new products in small quantities to gauge market interest and gather feedback. Based on the results, adjust your product offerings and scale up production as needed.

Planning For Long-Term Success

Planning for long-term success involves creating a strategic roadmap that ensures sustainable growth and resilience. Start by setting clear, long-term goals for your cricket farm. These goals should include financial targets, production milestones, and market expansion plans.

Develop a financial plan that includes budgeting for ongoing expenses, investments in infrastructure, and potential contingency funds. Regularly review your financial performance and adjust your budget as needed to stay on track with your growth objectives.

Implement a continuous improvement strategy. Regularly evaluate your processes, seek feedback from customers, and stay updated on industry trends. This proactive approach helps you adapt to changes in the market, innovate your offerings, and maintain a competitive edge.

Incorporate risk management practices into your long-term plan. Identify potential risks, such as supply chain disruptions or disease outbreaks, and develop contingency plans to address them. Building a strong network of suppliers, partners, and advisors can also provide additional support and resources for navigating challenges.

By following these steps, you can effectively expand and scale your cricket farm, ensuring long-term success and sustainability.

Frequently Asked Question And Their Answers

What is cricket farming? Cricket farming involves raising crickets in controlled environments for various purposes, including animal feed, human consumption, and bait. It focuses on breeding, rearing, and harvesting crickets efficiently.

Why farm crickets? Crickets are a sustainable protein source with a low environmental impact compared to traditional livestock. They require less land, water, and feed, making them an eco-friendly alternative for protein production.

What are the main benefits of crickets as a food source? Crickets are rich in protein, vitamins, and minerals. They also contain healthy fats and fiber. They are also considered a more sustainable and environmentally friendly protein source compared to traditional meat.

What are the basic requirements for starting a cricket farm? Essential requirements include a suitable space with controlled temperature and humidity, proper feeding equipment, a waste management system, and cricket containers or enclosures.

How do you set up a cricket farm? Start by selecting a suitable location, setting up cricket enclosures with appropriate temperature and humidity controls, providing feed and water, and ensuring good ventilation and sanitation.

What is the ideal temperature and humidity for raising crickets? Crickets generally thrive in temperatures between 80-90°F (27-32°C) and humidity levels of 40-60%. Specific needs can vary depending on the cricket species.

What do crickets eat? Crickets are omnivorous and can be fed a variety of diets, including commercial cricket feed, fruits, vegetables, grains, and protein supplements.

How often should you feed crickets? Crickets should be fed daily or every other day, depending on their growth stage and the type of feed. It's important to ensure they have constant access to food and fresh water.

How long does it take for crickets to reach maturity? Crickets typically take around 6-8 weeks from hatching to reach maturity, but this can vary based on species, temperature, and feeding conditions.

How do you manage waste in a cricket farm? Regular cleaning of enclosures, removal of waste and uneaten food, and proper ventilation are crucial. Using substrates that can absorb waste and facilitate easy cleaning helps manage waste effectively.

What diseases or pests are common in cricket farming? Common issues include fungal infections, mites, and parasites. Maintaining proper hygiene, controlling humidity, and regular monitoring can help prevent and manage these problems.

How do you harvest crickets? Crickets are usually harvested by removing them from their enclosures using specialized equipment. They are then sorted, cleaned, and processed for their intended use.

What are the main challenges in cricket farming? Challenges include maintaining optimal environmental conditions, managing diseases and pests, and ensuring a consistent and nutritious feed supply.

Can crickets be farmed indoors? Yes, crickets can be farmed indoors using controlled environments such as specialized insect-rearing facilities or dedicated rooms within existing buildings.

How do you ensure the quality of crickets for human consumption? To ensure quality, follow strict hygiene and sanitation practices, provide a balanced diet, and adhere to food safety regulations for harvesting and processing.

What are the legal considerations for cricket farming? Legal requirements vary by location and may include permits for animal farming, food safety regulations, and compliance with local zoning laws. Check with local authorities for specific requirements.

How can I market my crickets? Marketing can be done through local farmers' markets, online platforms, or by establishing partnerships with pet food companies, restaurants, or health food stores.

What are the environmental benefits of cricket farming? Cricket farming has a lower carbon footprint compared to traditional livestock farming.

Crickets require less water, land, and feed, and produce fewer greenhouse gases and waste.

How do crickets reproduce? Crickets reproduce through mating, where males and females mate, and females lay eggs on a suitable substrate. The eggs hatch into nymphs, which then mature into adult crickets.

Can cricket farming be profitable? Yes, cricket farming can be profitable if managed well. Factors influencing profitability include market demand, production costs, and efficient farm management practices.

CONCLUSION

Cricket farming represents a transformative leap in sustainable agriculture and food production. As global populations grow and the strain on traditional agricultural systems intensifies, alternative protein sources like crickets offer a promising solution to address the challenges of food security, environmental sustainability, and resource efficiency.

Crickets are remarkably efficient in converting feed into protein. They require significantly less land, water, and feed compared to conventional livestock. For instance, crickets can produce the same amount of protein as cattle with only a fraction of the resources, making them an attractive option for reducing the environmental footprint of our food systems.

Additionally, their rapid growth cycle and high reproductive rates further enhance their efficiency as a food source.

From a nutritional perspective, crickets are a powerhouse of essential nutrients. They provide high-quality protein, essential amino acids, vitamins, and minerals, making them a valuable addition to diets worldwide. Their ability to improve human nutrition, particularly in regions facing protein deficiency, underscores their potential to contribute to global food security.

Moreover, the integration of cricket farming into agriculture can promote biodiversity and soil health. Crickets can be reared using organic waste, which helps in recycling nutrients back into the ecosystem. This approach not only reduces waste but also supports sustainable farming practices.

However, the widespread adoption of cricket farming is not without challenges. Consumer acceptance remains a significant barrier, as cultural attitudes towards eating insects vary greatly across regions. Effective education and awareness campaigns are crucial to overcoming these barriers and fostering a broader acceptance of crickets as a mainstream food source. Additionally, regulatory frameworks and standards need to be established to ensure the safety and quality of cricket-based products.

The economic feasibility of cricket farming also requires attention. While initial setup costs and technology investments can be high, advancements in farming techniques and economies of scale are expected to reduce costs over time. As research and development continue to drive innovation in cricket farming, the industry is likely to become more cost-effective and accessible.

In conclusion, cricket farming holds immense potential to reshape the future of food production. Its environmental benefits, nutritional advantages, and capacity for sustainable growth make it a crucial component of a resilient and resource-efficient food system. Embracing cricket farming can lead to a more sustainable, equitable, and innovative approach to meeting the world's food needs. As we look toward the future, the integration of cricket farming into mainstream agriculture represents a promising step toward achieving global food security and sustainability.

THE END

www.ingramcontent.com/pod-product-compliance
Lightning Source LLC
Chambersburg PA
CBHW071835210526
45479CB00001B/140